VOL. 114

HAL•LEONARD®
GUITAR PLAY-ALONG

AUDIO
ACCESS
INCLUDED

BON JOVI

Page	Title
2	Bad Medicine
12	Have a Nice Day
18	In and Out of Love
26	It's My Life
32	Lay Your Hands on Me
43	Livin' on a Prayer
50	Runaway
57	Wanted Dead or Alive
64	GUITAR NOTATION LEGEND

PLAYBACK+
Speed • Pitch • Balance • Loop

To access audio visit:
www.halleonard.com/mylibrary

Enter Code
3634-2395-1176-0012

Bad Medicine

Words and Music by Jon Bon Jovi, Desmond Child and Richie Sambora

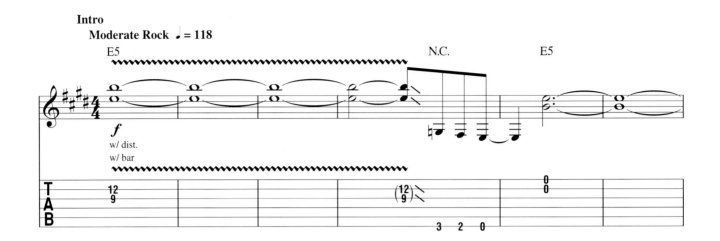

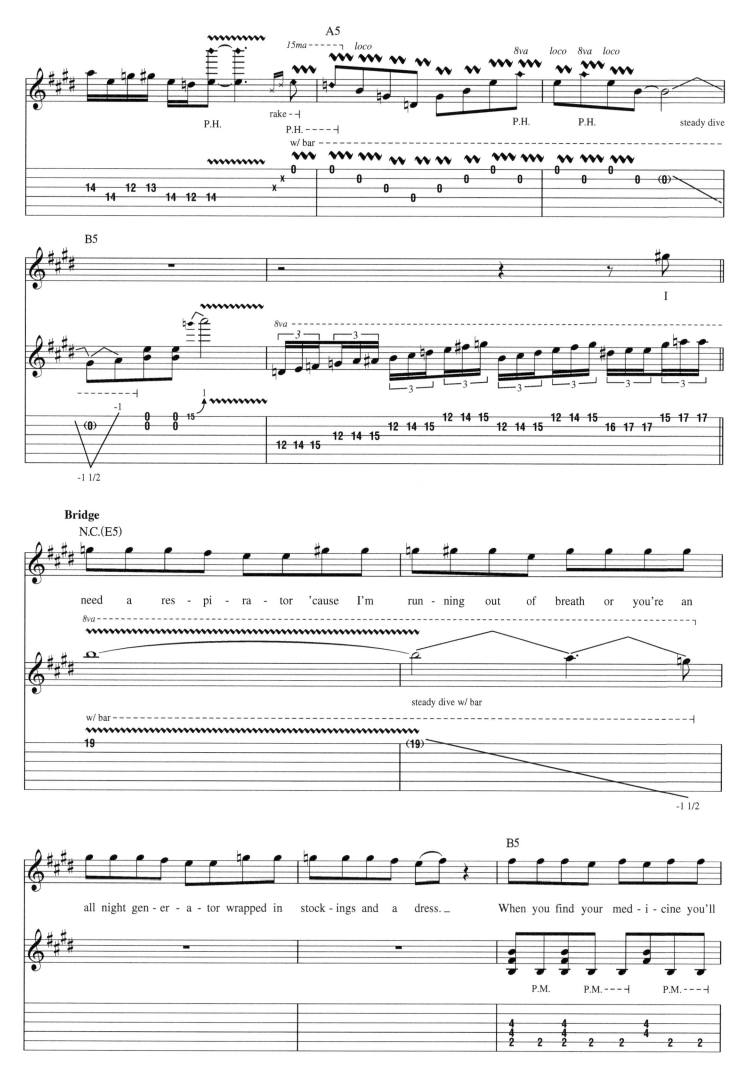

Interlude

F#5 E5

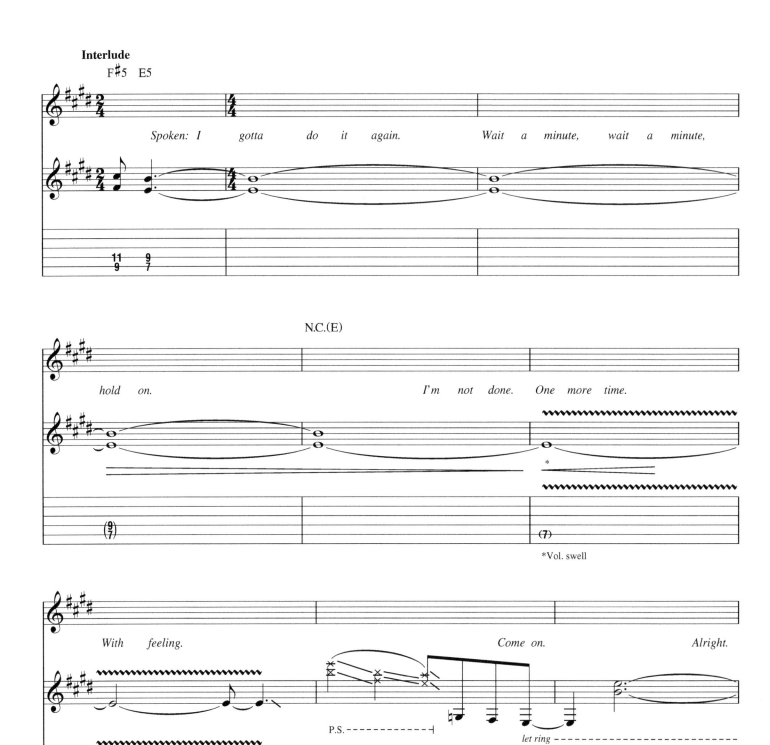

Spoken: I gotta do it again. Wait a minute, wait a minute,

N.C.(E)

hold   on.   *I'm not done. One more time.*

*Vol. swell

With   feeling.   *Come on.*   *Alright.*

P.S.

let ring

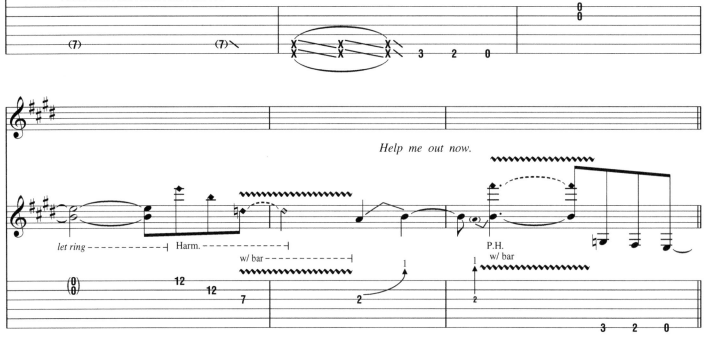

Help me out now.

let ring   Harm.

w/ bar

P.H.
w/ bar

Chorus

2nd time, substitute Fill 1

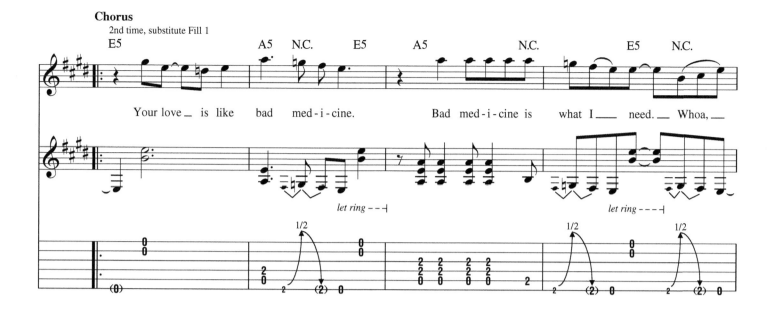

Your love __ is like bad med-i-cine. Bad med-i-cine is what I __ need. __ Whoa, __

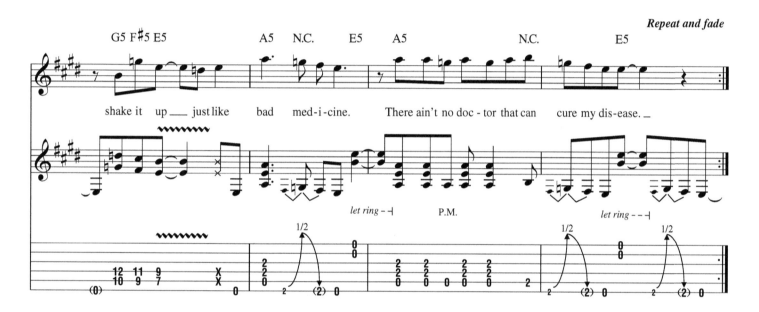

Repeat and fade

shake it up __ just like bad med-i-cine. There ain't no doc-tor that can cure my dis-ease. __

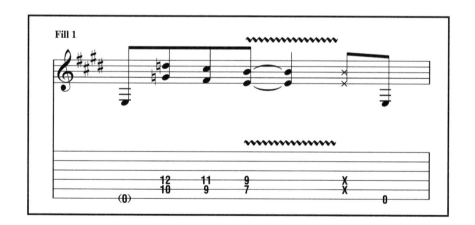

Fill 1

Additional Lyrics

2. I don't need no needle to be givin' me a thrill.
   And I don't need no anesthesia, or a nurse to bring a pill.
   I got a jones for your affection, like a monkey on my back.
   There ain't no paramedic gonna save this heart attack.
   When you need,...

Have a Nice Day

Words and Music by Jon Bon Jovi, Richie Sambora and John Shanks

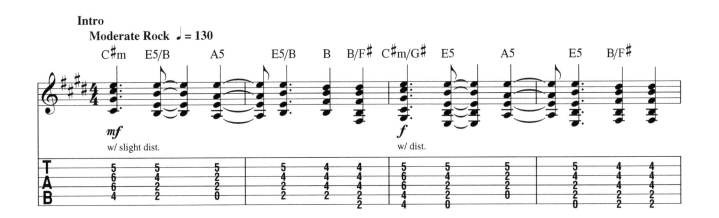

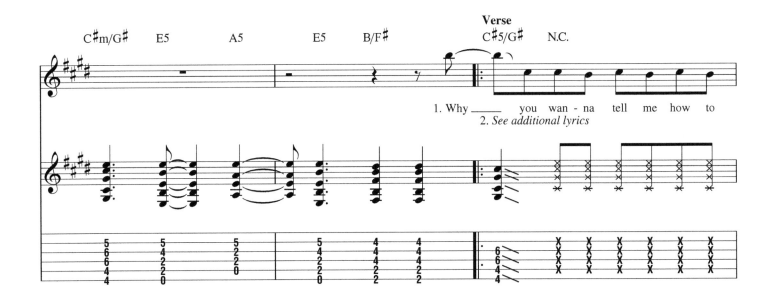

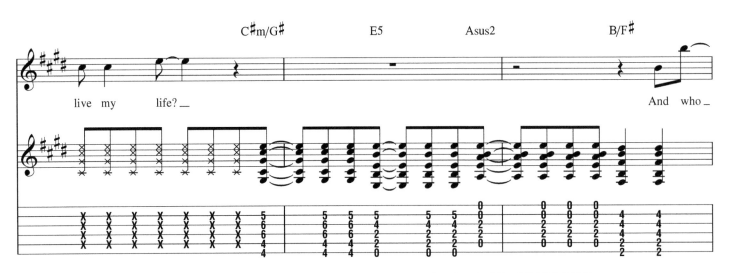

16

Outro

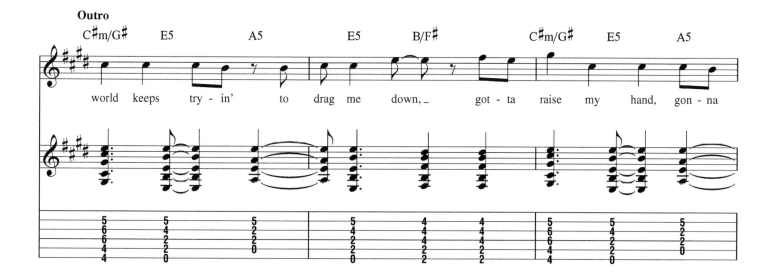

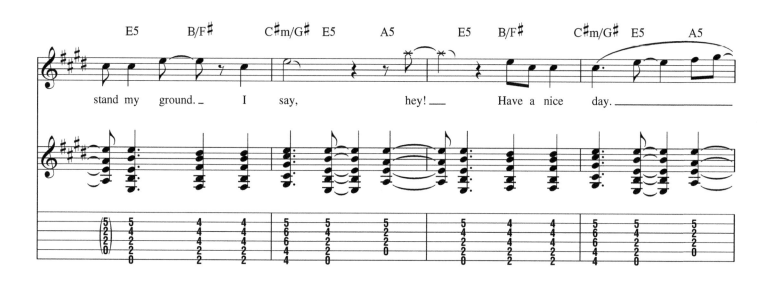

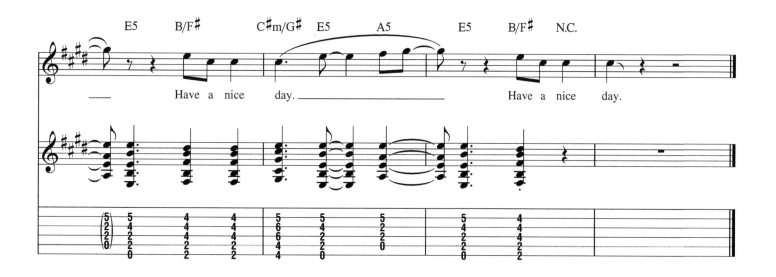

Additional Lyrics

2. Take a look around you; nothin's what it seems.
   We're livin' in the broken home of hopes and dreams.
   Let me be the first to shake a helpin' hand,
   Anybody brave enough to take a stand.
   I've knocked on ev'ry door down ev'ry dead-end street,
   Lookin' for forgiveness and what's left to believe.

In and Out of Love

Words and Music by Jon Bon Jovi

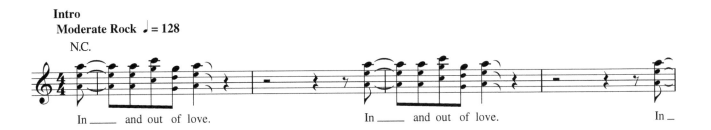

Guitar Solo

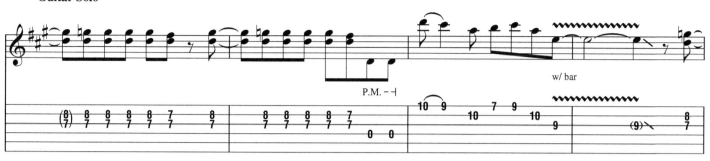

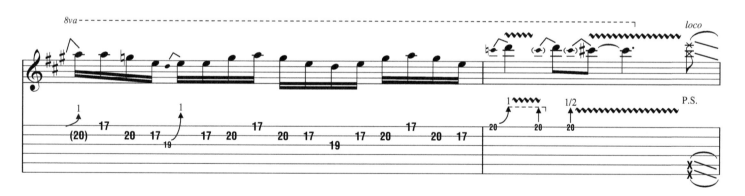

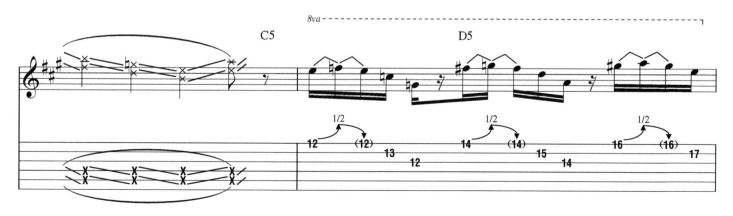

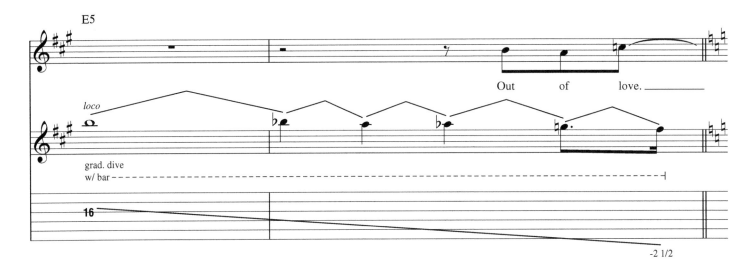

Bridge

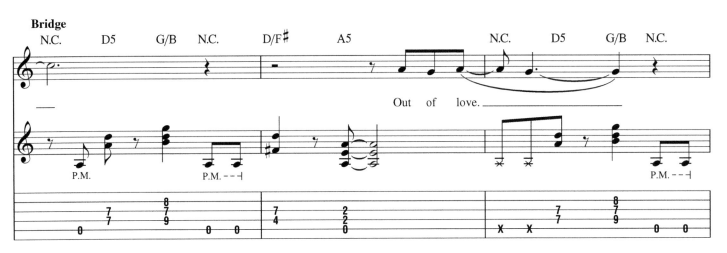

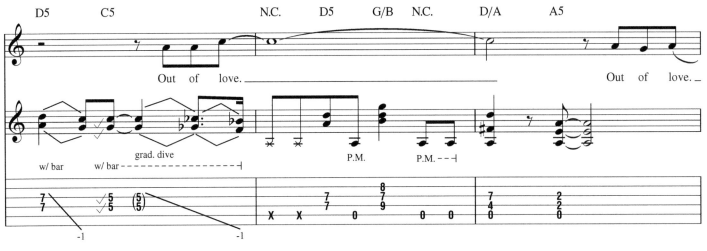

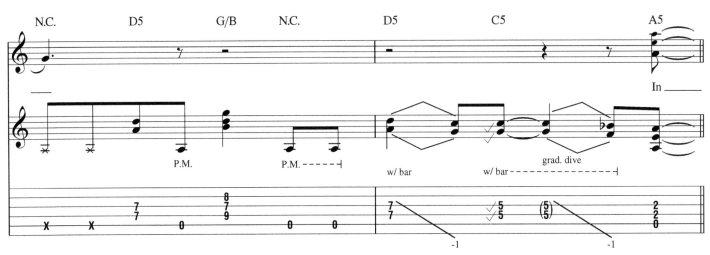

Breakdown

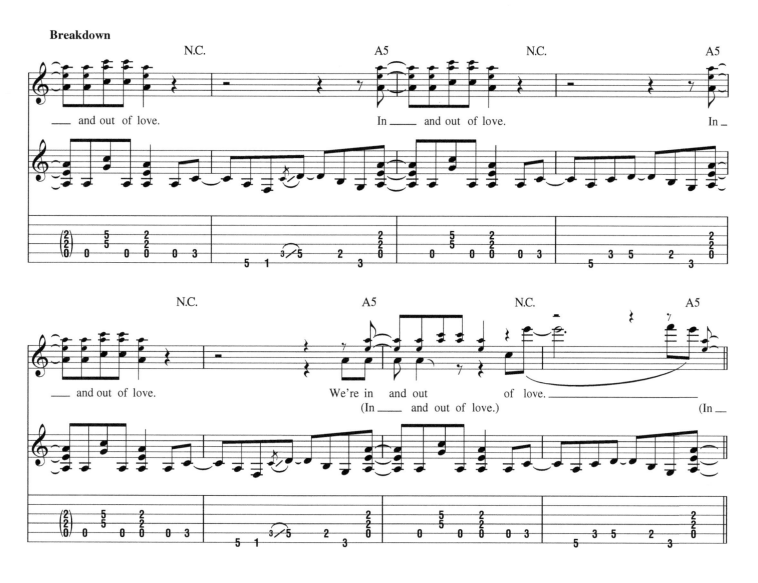

Outro-Chorus
w/ Lead Voc. ad lib.

Repeat and fade

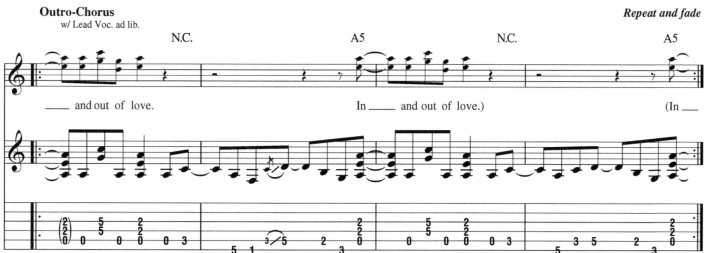

Additional Lyrics

    2. Running wild, when me and my boys hit the streets.
       Right on time, she's here to make my life complete.

Pre-Chorus Then I'm long gone, I got another show.
              One more time, one mile to go.
              One endless night of fantasy.
              It's all she left of her with me.

Chorus (In and out of love.) Hear what I'm saying.
        (In and out of love.) It's the way that we're playing.
        (In and out of love.) When we're together...

It's My Life

Words and Music by Jon Bon Jovi, Martin Sandberg and Richie Sambora

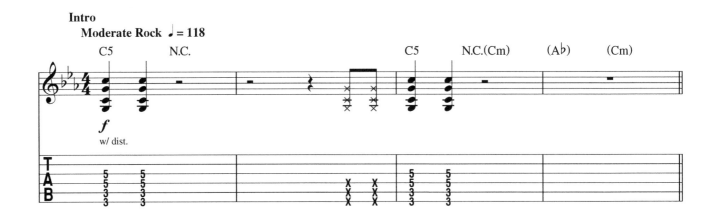

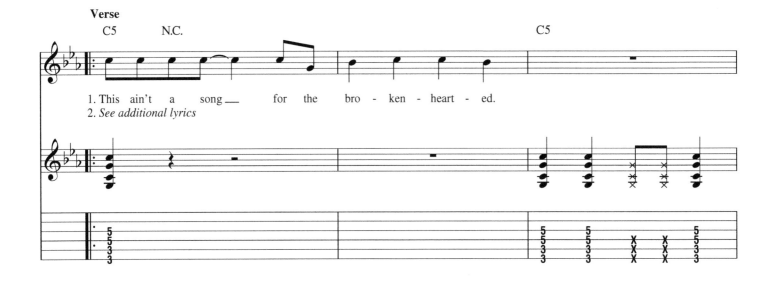

1. This ain't a song __ for the bro-ken-heart-ed.
2. *See additional lyrics*

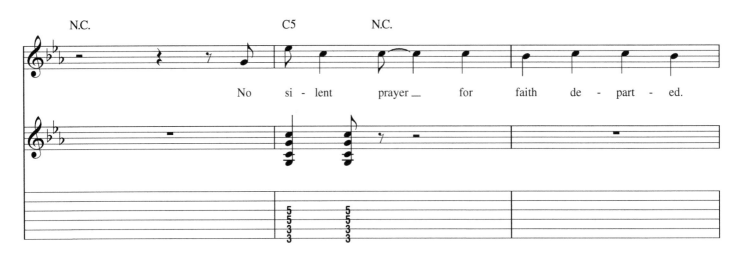

No si-lent prayer __ for faith de-part-ed.

2nd time, substitute Fill 1

And I ain't gon-na be just a face in the crowd. You're gon-na hear my voice when I shout it out loud.

Chorus

It's my life, it's now or nev-er.

Fill 1

Additional Lyrics

2. Yeah, this is for the ones who stood their ground,
For Tommy and Gina, who never backed down.
Tomorrow's gettin' harder, make no mistake.
Luck ain't even lucky, gotta make your own breaks.

Lay Your Hands on Me

Words and Music by Jon Bon Jovi and Richie Sambora

Drop D tuning:
(low to high) D-A-D-G-B-E

Intro
Moderately ♩ = 100

Lay ___ your hands on ___ me,

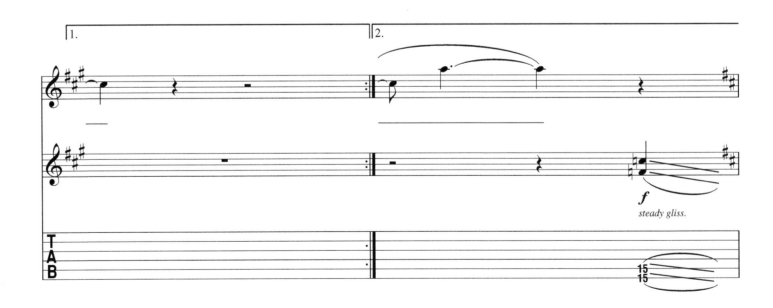

lay ___ your hands on ___ me, lay ___ your hands on ___ me. ___

steady gliss.

lay my ___ cards out on the ta - ble. You're

mine, and I'm yours for the tak - in'. Right now those

rules they made are meant ___ for ___ break - in'. _____

Pre-Chorus

N.C.(G7)

What you get ain't al - ways what you see, ___ but
See additional lyrics

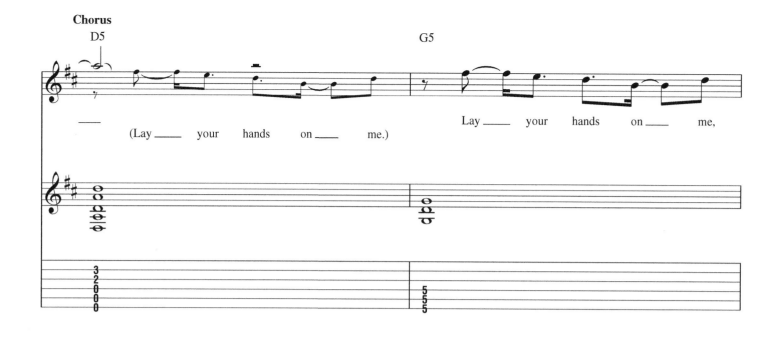

(Lay ____ your hands on ____ me.) Lay ____ your hands on ____ me,

lay ____ your hands on ____ me. ____ All you got to do ____ is

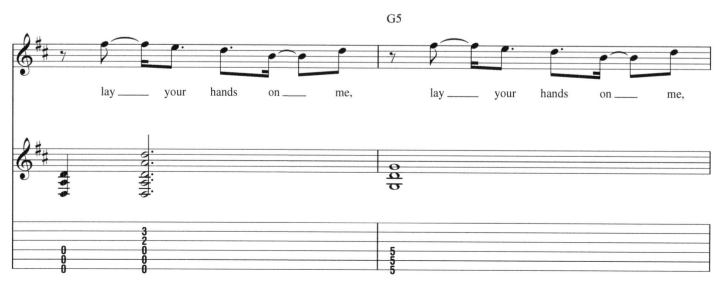

lay ____ your hands on ____ me, lay ____ your hands on ____ me,

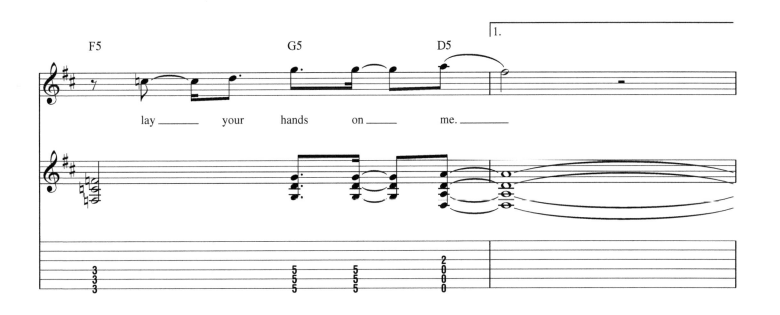

lay _____ your hands on _____ me. _____

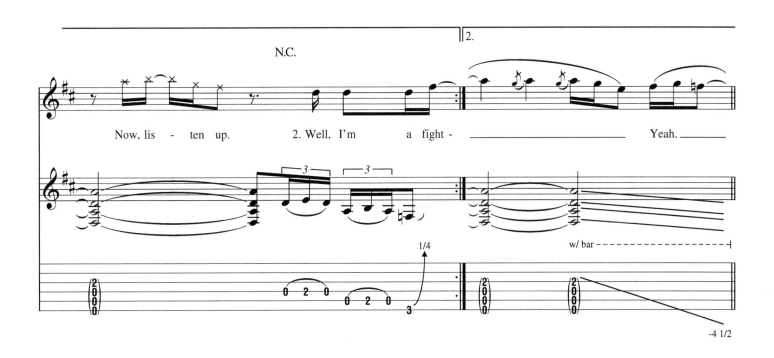

Now, lis - ten up.　　2. Well, I'm　　a fight - _____ Yeah. _____

Guitar Solo

D5　　Csus2　　D5　　N.C.

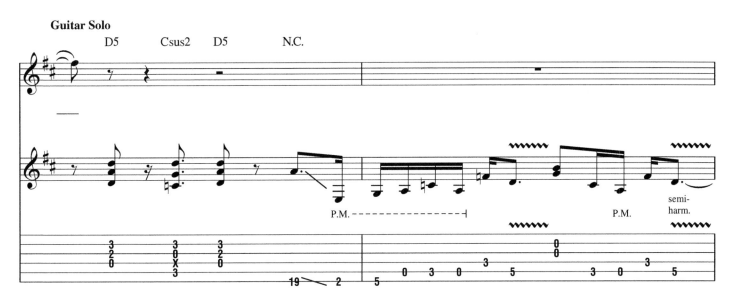

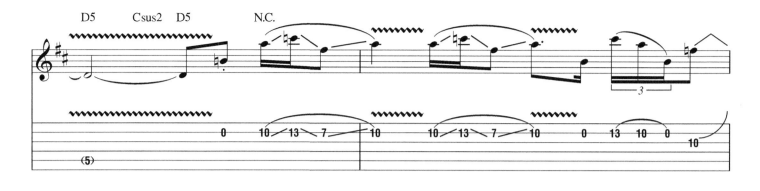

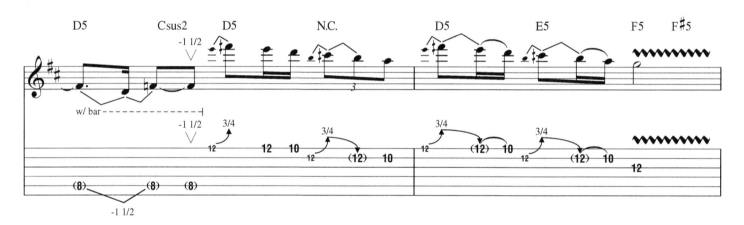

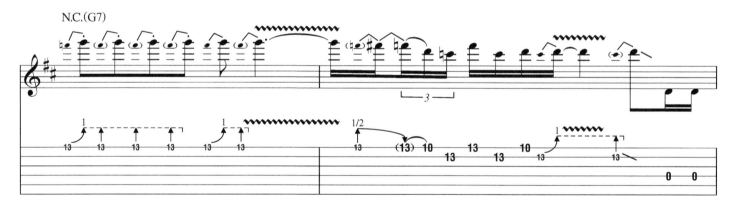

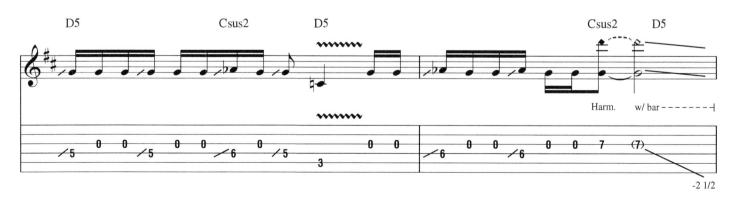

Interlude

Whoa, __ whoa. __

What-cha got-ta do __ is, lay 'em on me.

Well, come on, come on, come on. __

And ev-'ry-bod - y gon-na help me now. __ I can feel the peo-

- ple sing, I can feel my heart say - in', "If you want me,

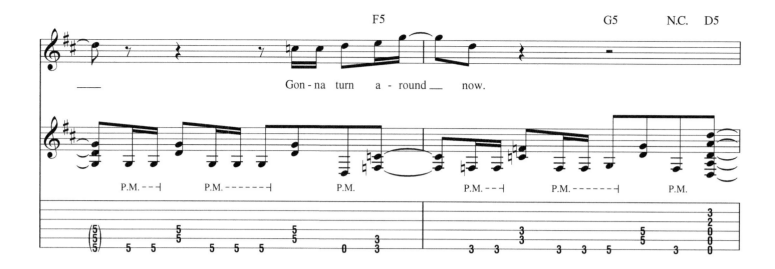

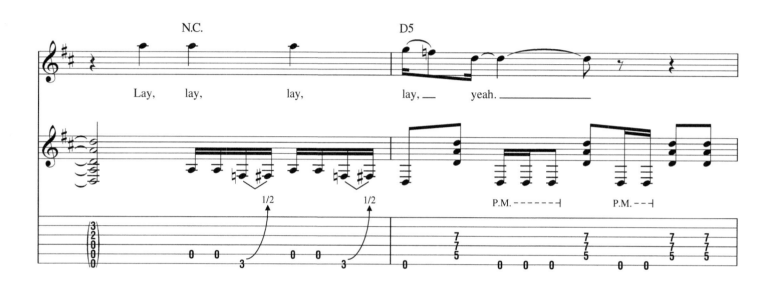

Additional Lyrics

2. Well, I'm a fighter, I'm a poet, I'm a preacher.
   I've been to school and baby, I've been the teacher.
   If you show me how to get up off the ground, ground, ground,
   I can show you how to fly and never ever come back down.

Pre-Chorus 2. Ev'rything you want is what I need.
   Your satisfaction is a, guaranteed.
   But the ride don't never, ever come for free, no, no, no, no, no.
   If you want me to lay my hands on you...

Livin' on a Prayer

Words and Music by Jon Bon Jovi, Desmond Child and Richie Sambora

Intro
Moderate Rock ♩ = 122

Spoken: Once   upon   a   time,

not so long ago...

Verse

1. Tom - my used to work on the docks. _____ Un - ion's been on strike, he's

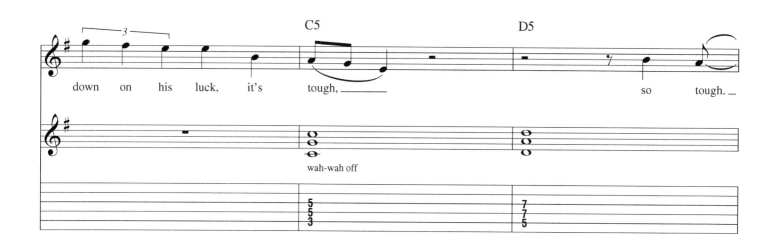

down on his luck, it's tough, _____ so tough. _

wah-wah off

Gi - na works the din - er all day. _

w/ wah-wah

Work - ing for her man, she brings home her pay for

love, _____ mm, for love. _____

wah-wah off

w/ wah-wah

𝄋 Pre-Chorus

She says we've got to hold on _____ to what we've got. It

wah-wah off

does-n't make a dif-f'rence if we make it or not. We've got each oth - er, and

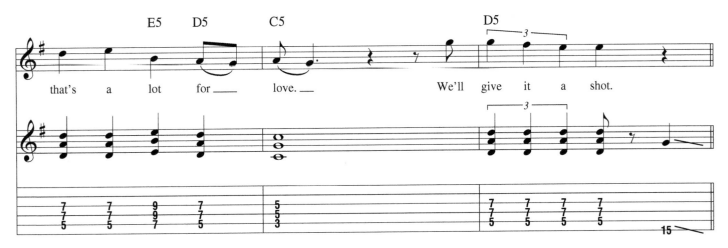

that's a lot for _____ love. _____ We'll give it a shot.

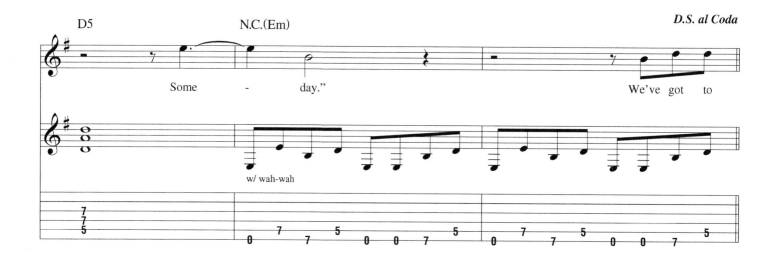

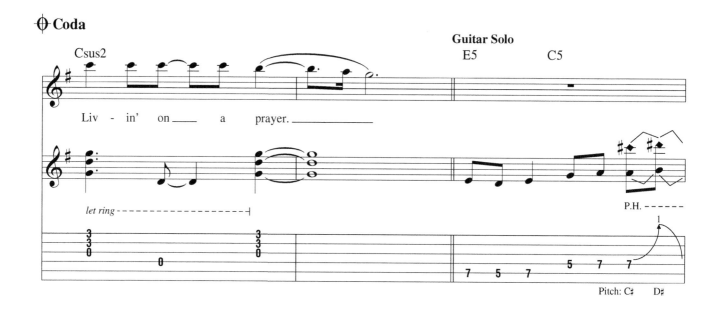

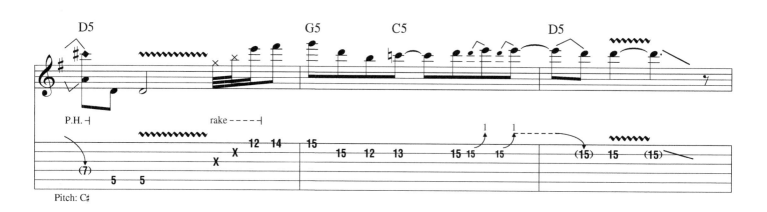

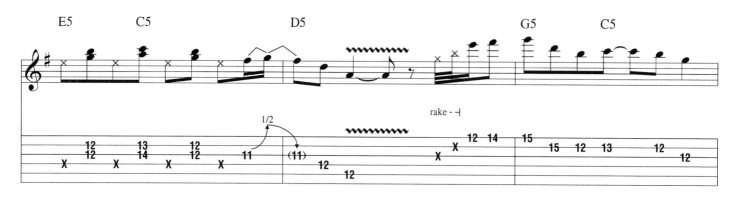

Runaway

Words and Music by Jon Bon Jovi and George Karakoglou

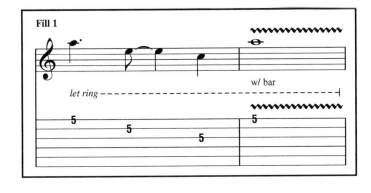
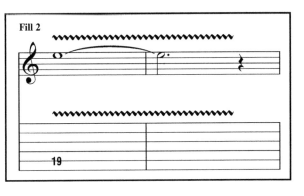

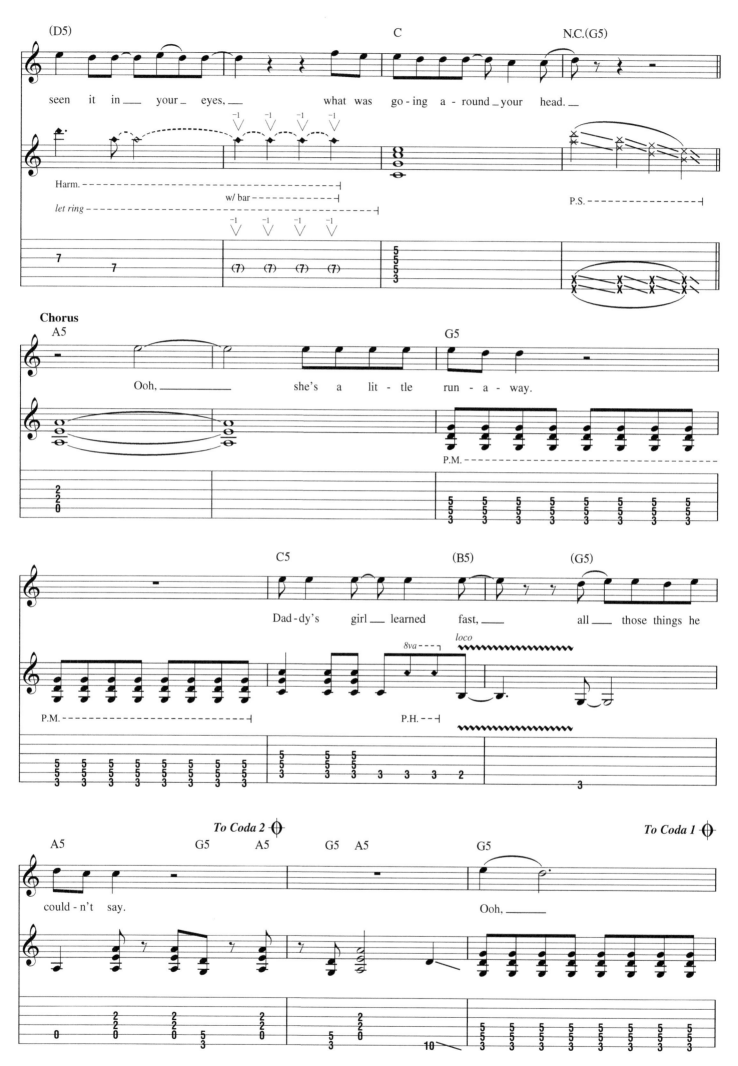

she's a lit - tle run - a - way.

Verse

2. Dif - f'rent line ev - 'ry night; guar - an - teed to blow your mind.

I see you out on the streets; call — me for a wild — time.

So you sit home a - lone 'cause there's noth - ing left that you can do.

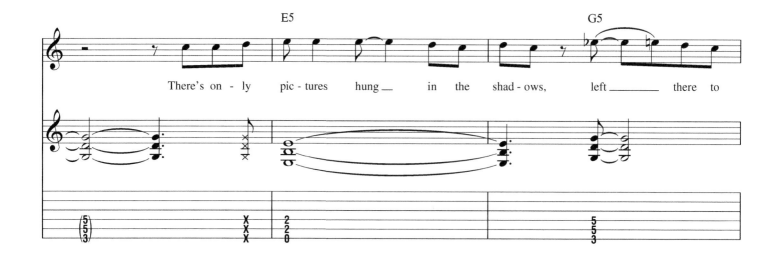

E5   G5

There's on - ly pic - tures hung ___ in the shad - ows, left _____ there to

D.S. al Coda 1

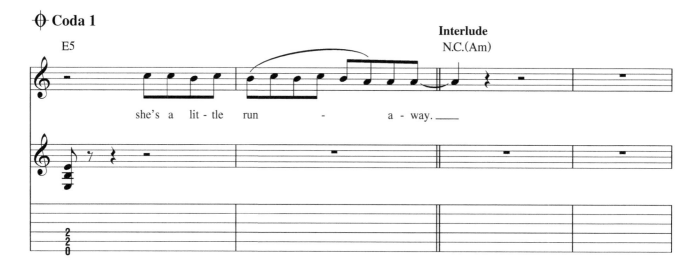

N.C.(Am)

look at you.

⊕ Coda 1

E5   **Interlude**
                                       N.C.(Am)

she's a lit - tle run - a - way. ___

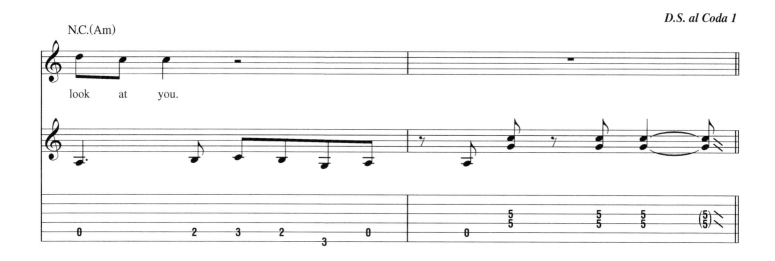

Guitar Solo

A5   A5

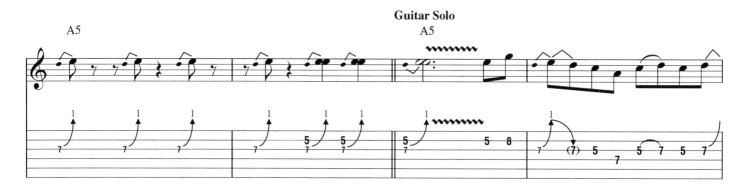

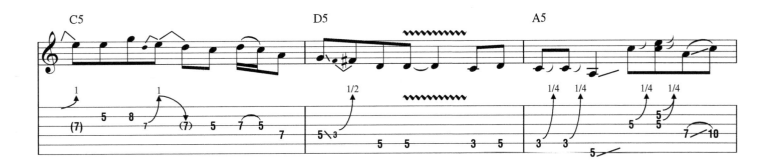

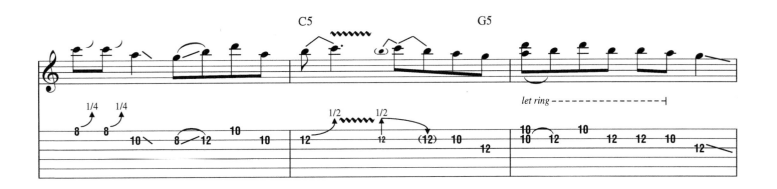

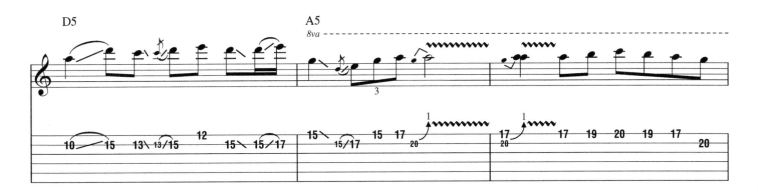

D.S. al Coda 2

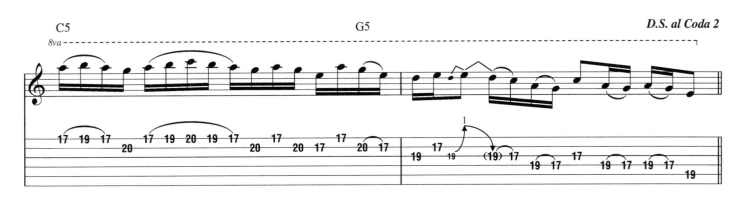

⊕ Coda 2

Chorus
w/ Voc. ad lib. on repeats

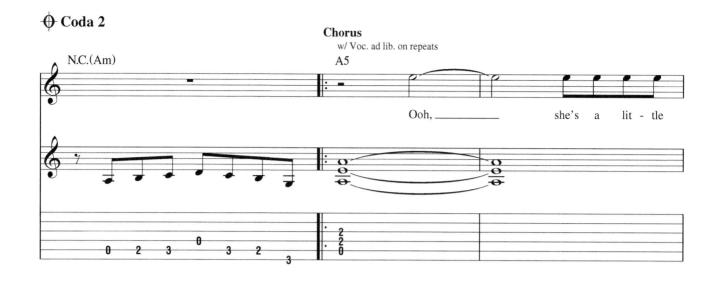

Ooh, _____ she's a lit - tle

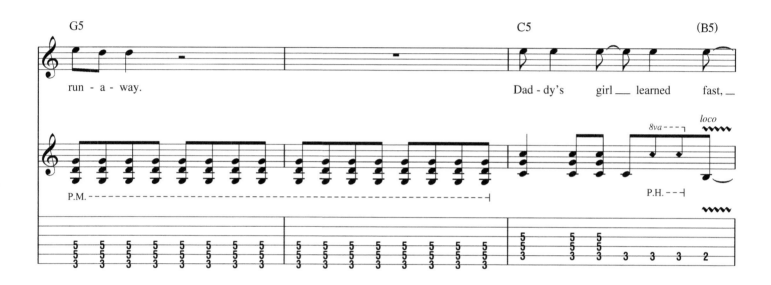

run - a - way. Dad - dy's girl ___ learned fast, ___

Repeat and fade

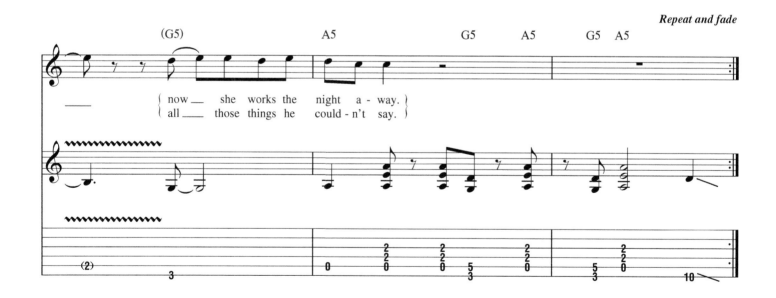

{ now ___ she works the night a - way. }
{ all ___ those things he could - n't say. }

Additional Lyrics

Pre-Chorus 2. You know she likes the lights at night
On the neon Broadway signs.
She don't really mind.
It's only love she hoped to find.

56

Wanted Dead or Alive

Words and Music by Jon Bon Jovi and Richie Sambora

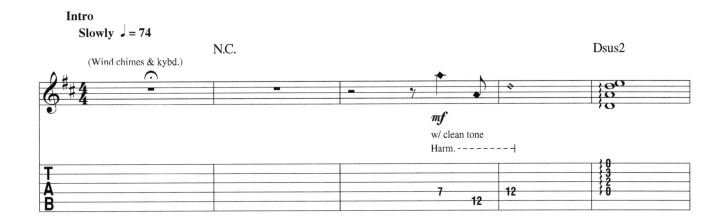

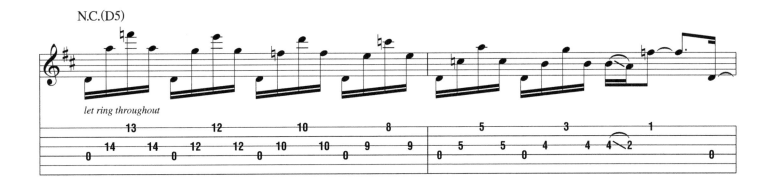

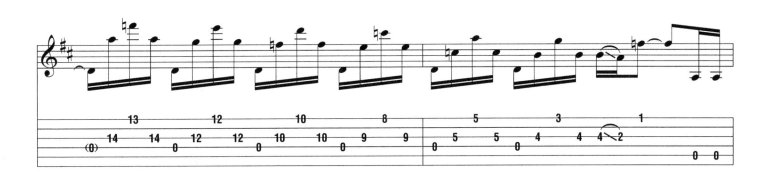

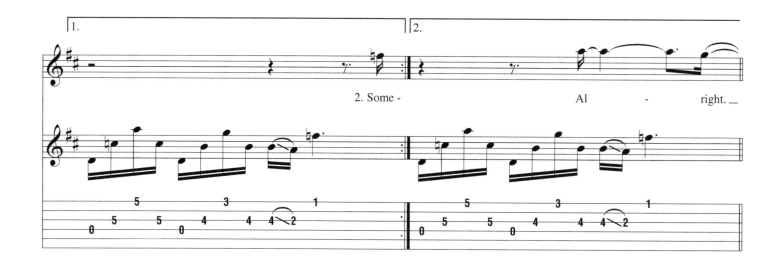

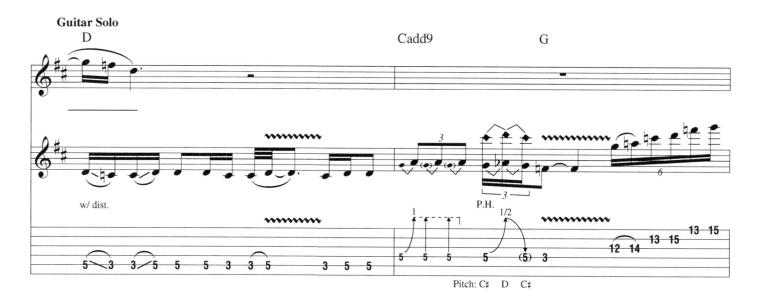

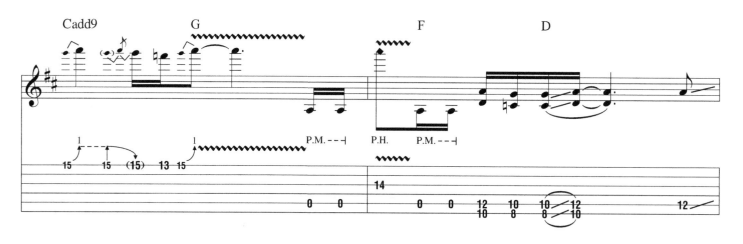

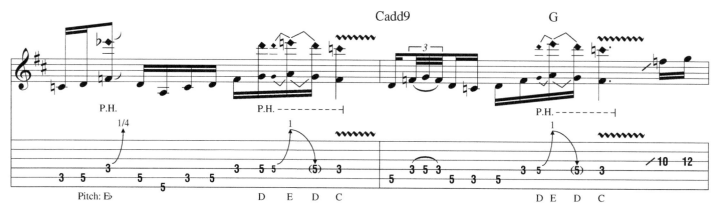

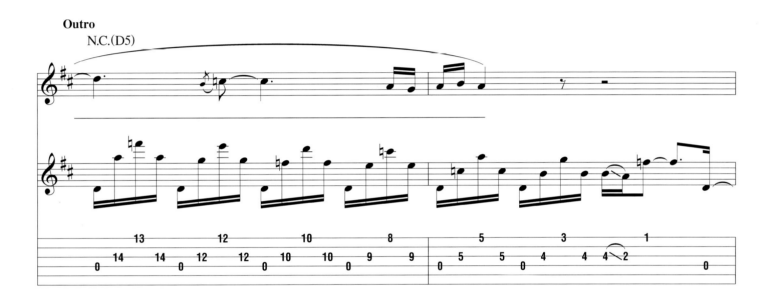

Outro

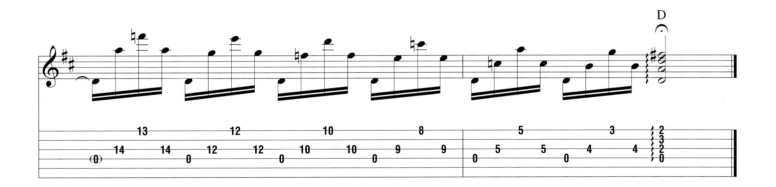

Additional Lyrics

2. Sometimes I sleep, sometimes it's not for days.
   The people I meet always go their sep'rate ways.
   Sometimes you tell the day by the bottle that you drink.
   And times when you're alone, all you do is think.

3. And I walk these streets, a loaded six-string on my back.
   I play for keeps, 'cause I might not make it back.
   I been ev'rywhere, still I'm standing tall.
   I've seen a million faces, and I've rocked them all.

Guitar Notation Legend

THE MUSICAL STAFF shows pitches and rhythms and is divided by bar lines into measures. Pitches are named after the first seven letters of the alphabet.

TABLATURE graphically represents the guitar fingerboard. Each horizontal line represents a string, and each number represents a fret.

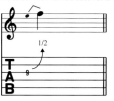

4th string, 2nd fret   1st & 2nd strings open, played together   open D chord

HALF-STEP BEND: Strike the note and bend up 1/2 step.

WHOLE-STEP BEND: Strike the note and bend up one step.

GRACE NOTE BEND: Strike the note and bend up as indicated. The first note does not take up any time.

SLIGHT (MICROTONE) BEND: Strike the note and bend up 1/4 step.

BEND AND RELEASE: Strike the note and bend up as indicated, then release back to the original note. Only the first note is struck.

PRE-BEND: Bend the note as indicated, then strike it.

VIBRATO: The string is vibrated by rapidly bending and releasing the note with the fretting hand.

PALM MUTING: The note is partially muted by the pick hand lightly touching the string(s) just before the bridge.

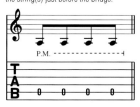

HAMMER-ON: Strike the first (lower) note with one finger, then sound the higher note (on the same string) with another finger by fretting it without picking.

PULL-OFF: Place both fingers on the notes to be sounded. Strike the first note and without picking, pull the finger off to sound the second (lower) note.

LEGATO SLIDE: Strike the first note and then slide the same fret-hand finger up or down to the second note. The second note is not struck.

SHIFT SLIDE: Same as legato slide, except the second note is struck.

TRILL: Very rapidly alternate between the notes indicated by continuously hammering on and pulling off.

TAPPING: Hammer ("tap") the fret indicated with the pick-hand index or middle finger and pull off to the note fretted by the fret hand.

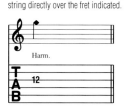

NATURAL HARMONIC: Strike the note while the fret-hand lightly touches the string directly over the fret indicated.

PINCH HARMONIC: The note is fretted normally and a harmonic is produced by adding the edge of the thumb or the tip of the index finger of the pick hand to the normal pick attack.

TREMOLO PICKING: The note is picked as rapidly and continuously as possible.

VIBRATO BAR DIVE AND RETURN: The pitch of the note or chord is dropped a specified number of steps (in rhythm) then returned to the original pitch.

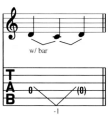

VIBRATO BAR SCOOP: Depress the bar just before striking the note, then quickly release the bar.

VIBRATO BAR DIP: Strike the note and then immediately drop a specified number of steps, then release back to the original pitch.

Additional Musical Definitions

(accent) • Accentuate note (play it louder)

(staccato) • Play the note short

D.S. al Coda • Go back to the sign (𝄋), then play until the measure marked ***"To Coda"***, then skip to the section labelled ***"Coda."***

D.C. al Fine • Go back to the beginning of the song and play until the measure marked ***"Fine"*** (end).

Fill • Label used to identify a brief melodic figure which is to be inserted into the arrangement.

N.C. • No Chord

  • Repeat measures between signs.

 • When a repeated section has different endings, play the first ending only the first time and the second ending only the second time.